FACE TO FACE WITH WOLVES

Jim and Judy Brandenburg

NATIONAL GEOGRAPHIC
WASHINGTON, D.C.

If you want to follow wolves in the wild, you have to think like a wolf.

FACE TO FACE

Wolves are very aware of their surroundings. Most of the time they are watching you before you see them.

I grew up on the flat and treeless prairie. That's where I first began dreaming about seeing a wild wolf. Wolves were my favorite animals as a boy, even though they were extinct on the prairie. I had seen them only in photos and paintings. When I was finally old enough to drive, I set out for the North Woods of Minnesota. I knew wolves still lived there, and I hoped to photograph one. But I could not find any in the deep, dense woods. They were there, of course, but I didn't know how to look for them.

WHAT BIG EYES YOU HAVE!

Throughout history, wolves have inspired both fear and admiration. They have been our hunting partners, our competitors, and our guides. This is why nearly every culture has folk stories about wolves.

- Fairy tales like Little Red Riding Hood reflect the fear that Europeans felt for wolves.

- In Rudyard Kipling's *The Jungle Book* and in the myth of Romulus and Remus, baby boys were raised by wolves.

- To some Native Americans, wolves were spirit guides who were revered for their hunting abilities.

Years later, I jumped at the chance to travel to the high Arctic, far north in Canada, for National Geographic. The white wolves there are usually not afraid of people, since they see so few humans. They are curious about us.

When I arrived on Ellesmere Island, just west of Greenland, I saw my first pack of seven white arctic wolves. I followed them as they headed toward an iceberg. The leader of the pack was the first to see me. He looked at me without fear, letting me know there was no way I would sneak up on him. He went on walking and climbing to what was clearly his favorite spot on the iceberg, a shelf halfway up. He sat down to watch me still clumsily trying to catch up to him. When I got as close to him as I could, we stared at each other. I looked at him through my powerful telephoto lens. After all these years, I was finally face to face with my favorite animal.

During that first summer, the wolves became used to seeing me around. I felt like I was part of the pack. I was able to follow them as they hunted musk oxen and then brought the food back to feed their pups, six cute little waddling gray bundles of fur. I watched the pups romp and play.

I left the Arctic after three summers, sad to go but excited, too. I would take what I had learned about wolf behavior and begin looking for gray wolves in my new home, the Boundary Waters Canoe Area Wilderness in northern Minnesota—the wolf country of my boyhood dreams. My wife and co-author, Judy, and I have lived in this beautiful, wild place for 30 years—with wolves for neighbors. 🐾

⬆ High on his iceberg throne, the leader of the pack surveys his territory. I named him Buster, after my father, the leader of my family's pack.

A young wolf pup explores his surroundings after his mother moved the pups to a new area, out in the open.

MEET THE WOLF

That photograph of the wolf on the iceberg turned out to be the most important picture I would ever make. I shot six frames before Buster left, but because of the cold, and my nervousness, only one turned out the way I hoped. Since then, I've learned more about wolves and how to gain their trust.

There are two species of wolves in North America: the red wolf and the most common, the gray wolf *(Canis lupus)*. Gray wolves live around the world, primarily in the northern climates.

A wolf howls to communicate with the rest of the pack. The sound can be heard many miles away.

9

The resident wolf pack in my backyard in Minnesota. Just 35 years ago, when I started photographing them, wolves were one of the most hated animals in the world. Today, they are one of the most loved. My photographs may have helped change attitudes—when you do something you care about, you can really make a difference!

Wolf families are called packs. The pack consists of a mother and father, called the alpha pair, and their offspring. The alpha female and alpha male are the leaders of the pack. The pups usually stay with the pack for two or three years. When they are grown, one of them might become the pack leader—or the alpha pair might drive them away. They then become lone wolves, who may someday join with other lone wolves to mate and form new packs.

The average wolf pack is 6 to 8 wolves. A pack of 20 wolves, including 5 pups, recently lived near me in northern Minnesota. This unusually large pack eventually split. The alpha pair remained nearby, and the new pack went off to set up its own territory. Wolves are territorial. They will travel great distances, about 30 miles (48 km) a day, to patrol their boundaries and to find food.

⬇ Wolves used to live all over the world, in North America, Asia, and Europe. The map below shows the range of the gray and red wolf species today. (The arctic wolf is a subspecies of gray.)

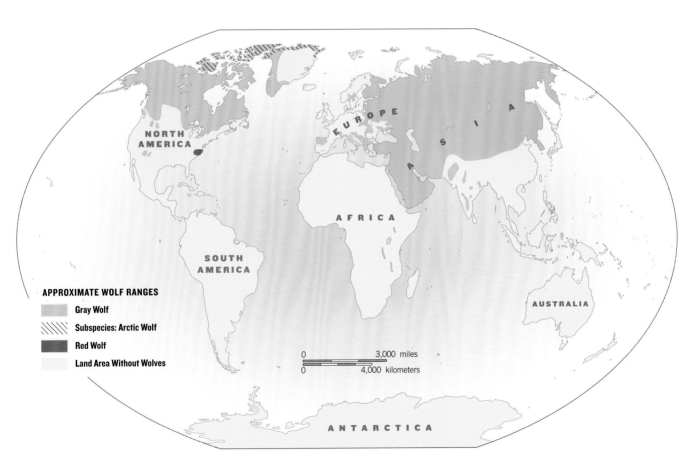

APPROXIMATE WOLF RANGES

Gray Wolf

Subspecies: Arctic Wolf

Red Wolf

Land Area Without Wolves

0   3,000 miles
0   4,000 kilometers

→ Wolves seem to be always on the move, mostly searching for food. But they are also on the lookout for danger. They can be killed if they wander into another pack's territory. Humans, and their traps, pose another threat.

↑ The low spring sun highlights the thick winter fur of this arctic wolf.

The coloration of a gray wolf can range from black to white, with many shades of a blondish, gray-brown in between.

HOW TO SPEAK WOLF

Wolves are famous for howling, but they communicate in lots of other ways, too. They growl, whimper, and use body language.

- A wolf greeting a more dominant animal slinks along the ground and sometimes rolls over on its back. The dominant wolf holds its tail high.

- To show affection, wolves lick each other's muzzles or wag their tails.

- When a wolf stares another wolf in the eye, it's a sign of aggression.

Wolves are social animals, which means they live and cooperate with other wolves. They have many ways to communicate. Smells, sounds, facial expressions, and body language can relay messages.

A wolf howl is one of nature's most interesting sounds. Wolves greet one another, show their location, and define their territory by howling. They can track the rest of the pack and warn off others.

Wolves sleep as much as 12 hours at a time. Upon waking, one wolf howls to the others to wake them up. The rest of the adults slowly get up, stretch, bow to each other, howl, and then depart on their hunt. I love being awakened at night by the sound of a wolf pack howling nearby.

← Pups love to join the rest of the pack in howling, but do so at a higher pitch.

LIFE IN THE PACK

S cientists often compare the wolf pack to a human family, because wolves live together and care for one another, just like humans. The wolf pack in my backyard has often seemed like family to me. This spring, when I realized that two of the pack's wolf pups had died, I felt the loss strongly.

Each year, around April or May, the alpha female usually bears one litter of four to six pups. Wolf pups weigh one pound (0.5 kg) at birth and are blind, deaf, and completely dependent on their mother.

← The pack often leaves the pups in the care of a baby-sitter. This wolf's job is not just to play with and protect them, but to teach important lessons about being a wolf.

15

They live in a hole or cave that the alpha pair finds or has dug in the ground. This first home is called a den. The pups stay in or near the den until they are about two months old and big enough to travel. Then the adults take them to a new place. This larger, open area, known as a rendezvous site, gives the growing pups more room to explore and sleep. The pups are moved often, and the sites are usually located near food and water sources.

Wolf pups love to play; they stalk, pounce, wrestle, and chew on each other. This is good practice for when they are old enough to go along

⬇ The alpha pair always eats first, then the subordinates eat. The wolf with the least status, the omega wolf, eats last.

on hunts with the pack. During play, the pups find out who is the most dominant. This is very important for the stability of the family.

Every adult in the wolf pack will help take care of the pups by bringing them food and playing with them. When most of the pack is out hunting, one adult—the babysitter—usually stays with the pups. Sometimes, if the pack is small, the adults may have to leave the pups alone while they hunt. This leaves the pups vulnerable to other predators, such as bears.

The pack will also share in caring for elder or injured members of the pack. I've watched the pack near my home take care of a wolf I call Broken Foot.

⬆ Born with black fuzzy fur, pups nurse (right) until they are about six weeks old.

Much tenderness is shown between the alpha pair during courtship (left).

⬆ An adult wolf (left) shows the alpha male it accepts its higher status by displaying submissive body language.

Wolves howl (right) at different pitches to create discord. The pack then appears much larger to other wolf packs in the area.

One of his front paws was clearly broken and never healed, most likely from a steel trap. For the last three years, he has hopped along on three legs. Other wolves in his pack greet him and show him respect, letting him eat with the pack. Because of his broken foot, he cannot go on a hunt for large animals. But he can hunt small animals like mice by pouncing on them and pinning them.

Wolves are good at catching and killing large animals. They can run very fast, from 25 to 40 miles an hour (40–65 km/h) for short distances. Their powerful jaws and interlocking teeth help

← Hungry pups nip and nuzzle at an adult's mouth to stimulate regurgitation.

them catch and hang on to their prey. A wolf pack works together to hunt large prey such as deer, moose, caribou, musk oxen, bison, and elk. A lone wolf will seek out smaller animals like beaver, rabbits, and rodents, which are easier to catch.

To be healthy, each wolf should have about 2.5 pounds (1.1 kg) of food a day, so wolves must hunt often to catch enough food for the pack. They tend to prey on the sick, weak, injured, old, or young. When hunting is poor, wolves can go for long periods without eating. Especially for pups, starvation is one of the main causes of death. 🐾

HUNGRY LIKE A WOLF

As predators, wolves actually help deer and other herds stay healthy.

- **Wolfing food:** Wolves tend to prey on animals that are weak. They are easiest to catch!

- **Wolf workout:** The strong, healthy animals are the ones that get away. They survive and reproduce.

- **Cry for the wolf:** When wolves disappear from an area, deer and other animal populations get too numerous and soon suffer from hunger or disease.

A volunteer carries a sedated pup in Yellowstone National Park, Wyoming. The pup, which came from Canada, would eventually be released into the park.

MAKING A COMEBACK

In the early 1970s, there were fewer than 1,000 gray and red wolves left in the lower 48 states. To protect wolves from further decline, they were two of the first species given protection under the Endangered Species Act of 1973.

Since then, the wolf has made a remarkable recovery. How many wolves are there now in the world? Some estimates show more than 5,000 wolves in the lower 48 states, including 2,000 in Minnesota, and 7,000 to 12,000 in Alaska. Worldwide,

An arctic wolf jumps from one ice floe to another in search of scraps of food washed up from the sea.

A wolf reintroduced to Yellowstone National Park in Wyoming chases after a herd of elk.

there are at least 150,000 in 57 different countries.

Scientists have many ongoing studies of the wolf. The longest study of the wolf-and-prey relationship is at Isle Royale National Park on Lake Superior, where scientists have been observing wolves and their relationship with moose for 50 years.

In 1995 and 1996, wild wolves from Canada were released, or reintroduced, in the northern Rocky Mountains of Yellowstone National Park and in Idaho. Yellowstone is now the best place to see and hear wild wolves.

Local ranchers were opposed to the wolf reintroductions and threatened to shoot them to prevent
them from attacking livestock. A group called
Defenders of Wildlife worked out a compromise.
They established a fund to pay farmers and ranchers for livestock that the wolves killed. However,
it's not always clear how the livestock died. Wolves
often eat animals that have died from other causes.

America's wolves still need our help. Some
people want to change the wolves' status. In
Minnesota, wolf populations have begun to recover.

Here I am, following wolf
tracks and hoping to find
a wolf pack in Minnesota's
Boundary Waters Canoe Area
Wilderness.

23

Once highly endangered, wolves have made a remarkable recovery over the past 25 years. Here, a lone wolf howls to find his pack on Ellesmere Island, Canada.

Wolves in this state are no longer on the endangered species list.

In Alaska, where wolves were never endangered, they are hunted from airplanes. And new laws in Montana and Idaho allow hunters to kill hundreds of wolves. Environmental groups are speaking out against this change. Why is there a rush to kill these wolves? One reason is that wolves are often blamed for the decline in populations of elk and other animals hunted for sport, even though these declines may be also caused by natural events, like drought, or even human hunters.

People's fear and misunderstanding of wolves is the biggest threat to their survival. I hope that this attitude will change, and the howl of the wolf will again be heard in places it used to call home. 🐾

HOW YOU CAN HELP

⬇ Two young wolf pups play tug-of-war with a piece of fur from an arctic fox.

Humans and wolves in North America have had a long, tangled relationship. Many Native American tribes respected and revered wolves. But European settlers had a different view. As settlers pushed west in the 1800s, they came into conflict with wolves, who sometimes hunted their domestic animals. The federal government began paying hunters a bounty—a sum of money—for every wolf they killed. Wolves were shot, poisoned, and trapped to the brink of extinction.

That view of wolves has changed. Wolves were added to the endangered species list in 1973, and since then, wolf populations have made a comeback.

But some hunters and ranchers continue to oppose wolf reintroductions and laws that protect wolves. They blame wolves for a decline in deer herds, even though the decline could be caused by other factors, including drought, disease, and overhunting by humans. Other people think wolves are dangerous to humans, but healthy wild wolves have rarely attacked humans in North America Wolves are legally hunted in Alaska, and other states are trying to pass laws to allow hunting.

Here's how you can help:

■■ Be a wolf ambassador. Help to educate others about the important role wolves play in the ecosystem. Remind them that in modern times, there is not a single proven case of a wild, healthy wolf killing a person in the U.S.

■■ Learn about organizations like Defenders of Wildlife, the Wolf Conservation Center, and the International Wolf Center, which protect wild wolves.

■■ You and your friends or family could "adopt" a wolf from Wolf Song of Alaska or Defenders of Wildlife. In return, you might get a certificate or a wolf toy. Plus, you'll feel good knowing that you are helping protect wolves.

■■ Write to your representatives in Congress, especially if you live in a state that has wolves. Tell them that wild wolves are important to you and you want them protected.

IT'S YOUR TURN

Unless you live in the northern woods of Minnesota like Jim Brandenburg, you may have a hard time finding wolves in the wild. Here are some ideas for how you can enjoy wolves:

1 You might get a chance to see a wolf—or hear their haunting howls—if your family takes a trip to Yellowstone National Park in Wyoming. You could also see a wolf at a zoo or wildlife park. Some zoos keep wolves in family groups, where you can see them interact. How would the behavior of captive wolves be different from that of wild ones? How would it be the same?

2 There are many websites where you can listen to wolf howls. Try www.pbs.org/wgbh/nova/wolves/howl.html

3 Pay attention to the body language of the family dog. Wild wolves are its ancestors! Just like wolves, dogs roll over on their backs to show submission to a dominant member of their pack, wave their tails in greeting, and bow down and slap the ground with their forelegs when they want to play.

4 Curl up with a good book. You might like *Julie of the Wolves* by Jean Craighead George. This classic story is about a young girl who spends a season living with a family of arctic wolves. What typical wolf behaviors are described?

5 *Never Cry Wolf* is a movie about a wolf biologist who goes to the Arctic to solve the mystery of why caribou are dying. Based on a true story, it helped to dispel myths about wolves and to change people's attitudes toward them.

⬇ As pups grow, they become very curious about their surroundings.

FACTS AT A GLANCE

⬇ An arctic wolf rests in a field of cotton grass after a long hunt; wolves sometimes sleep 12 hours straight.

Scientific and Common Names

The species name for the gray wolf is *Canis lupus*. The gray wolf has five subspecies in North America: the arctic wolf, the eastern timber wolf, the Rocky Mountain or Mackenzie Valley wolf, the Mexican wolf, and the Great Plains wolf. All canines (wolves, dogs, foxes, jackals, and coyotes) belong to a group of animals called Carnivora, which also includes bears, seals, and other predators.

Types of Wolves

There are two wolf species: gray and red. (Another animal, the Ethiopian wolf, is considered a third, separate species of wolf by many scientists. However, others argue that it is just related to wolves, like a jackal or coyote is.) At least 150,000 gray wolves exist; they are not endangered. Red wolves, native to the southeastern United States, are critically endangered, with fewer than 150 animals.

Size

Gray wolves are the largest canines in the wild, standing 26–32 inches (66–81 cm) tall at the shoulder. On average, females weigh about 80 pounds (36 kg); males about 90 pounds (41 kg).

Life Spans

It's tough being a wolf. Young wolves die from starvation or are killed by predators like bears, coyotes, or other wolves. Grown wolves can starve or suffer from diseases, be killed by hunters, be hit by cars, or be injured by the flying hooves of their prey. The average wild wolf lives six to eight years. Captive wolves can live for twice as long.

Special Features

Wolves are intelligent and highly social creatures. They communicate through sound, scent marking, and body language. Within the pack, social status determines which wolves get such privileges as eating first or mating. Groups of wolves hunt cooperatively to capture prey.

Habitat and Range

Wolves used to live in northern

Map A: Historic Range

Map B: 1973 Range

Map C: Current Range

latitudes around the world. They are adapted to many environments, including prairie, woods, desert, and Arctic regions. Now they live mainly in remote wilderness areas in Canada, the northern United States, and parts of Europe and Asia.

Food

Wolves hunt a variety of prey, from huge caribou and moose to tiny field mice. Occasionally, they are scavengers, eating animals that are already dead. Sometimes wolves kill cattle and sheep, leading to conflicts with humans. Wolves live in a perpetual cycle of feasting and famine. A wolf can gulp 20 pounds (9 kg) of meat at a sitting, or it can go two weeks without eating.

Reproduction

Wolves usually live in family groups consisting of an alpha pair of wolves who reproduce, and several other wolves who may be grown offspring from previous years or other relatives. Wolves mate between January and May, depending on where they live, and the pups are born after a 60-day gestation (pregnancy). Pups don't open their eyes until they are two weeks old. They usually come out of the den for the first time at three weeks of age. They join the pack on the hunt when they are about six months old.

Biggest Threats

Because wolves need large territories in order to find enough food, habitat loss is a serious

Before Europeans settled the U.S., gray wolves lived in most of the country (Map A). By 1973, when they were listed as endangered, gray wolves were practically extinct in the U.S., living only in a limited area of northeastern Minnesota and Michigan's Isle Royale (Map B). Today, gray wolf populations are recovering as a result of their protected status and their reintroduction to selected areas (Map C).

problem for them. So is illegal killing by human hunters and ranchers. Where the needs of wolves and humans conflict, humans are the biggest threat that wolves have.

FIND OUT MORE

Books & Articles

Brandenburg, Jim. *Brother Wolf.* Minnetonka, MN: NorthWord, 1993.

Brandenburg, Jim. *Scruffy: A Wolf Finds His Place in the Pack.* New York, NY: Walker, 1996.

Brandenburg, Jim. *To the Top of the World: Adventures With Arctic Wolves.* New York, NY: Walker, 1993.

Brandenburg, Jim. *White Wolf.* Minnetonka, MN: NorthWord, 1988.

George, Jean Craighead. *Julie of the Wolves.* New York, NY: HarperCollins, 1972.

Websites

kids.nationalgeographic.com/animals
Check out the National Geographic pages on wolves.

kids.nationalgeographic.com/explore/nature/mission-animal-rescue
Learn how to help save wolves and other endangered animals.

defenders.org
Find information about wolves' biology and about conservation.

fws.gov/midwest/wolf/aboutwolves/biologue.htm
The U.S. Fish and Wildlife Service maintains a website on wolves that covers their history, *the reintroduction effort, and their recovery.*

wwf.org
The World Wildlife Fund has information on wolves and more!

howlingforwolves.org
Howling for Wolves, a Minnesota-based organization, offers the latest news and information on conservation for wolves.

endangered.org/wolves
Find an interactive map with wolves' statuses under the Endangered Species Act in each U.S. state.

EDUCATIONAL EXTENSIONS

Reading

1. What are some characteristics of wolf packs that make them similar to human families?

2. How did the Endangered Species Act of 1973 help wolf populations recover in the United States? What new issues arose as a result?

3. The authors give many reasons why we don't need to fear "the big bad wolf" and encourage us to be wolf advocates. How do their face to face experiences with wolves help to support their belief that wolves need to be protected?

Writing

4. Write a narrative essay about a time when you felt as though you were face to face with a wolf. You may have seen a wolf in a zoo or on a TV program, or you may even have read about one in another book. Describe your experience based on how you felt and what you were thinking, using dialogue effectively when needed. If you have never felt like you were face to face with a wolf before, use your imagination to tell a story about what you think it would be like.

Speaking & Listening

5. In small groups, have a collaborative discussion about the reintroduction of wolves to areas that they used to inhabit. Have some of your classmates or friends present the arguments for helping wolf populations recover, and have the others present the arguments of local ranchers and hunters who oppose reintroduction.

GLOSSARY

Alpha: The highest-ranking wolf in a pack.

Den: A burrow in the ground or in a cave where wolf mothers give birth and nurse their pups. Adults don't sleep in the den.

Endangered species: A species with very few individuals remaining. If the number of individuals rises, the classification may change to "threatened" or "recovered." If the number falls, the species may become "extinct," meaning no individuals are left.

Habitat: The local environment in which an animal lives.

Mammals: Air-breathing, warm-blooded animals with hair whose offspring nurse on their mother's milk.

Omega: The lowest-ranking wolf in a pack.

Predator: An animal that preys on other animals as food.

Prey: Animals that predators eat.

Species: A group of animals or plants that look similar, can breed with one another, and have offspring who can also breed successfully.

Subspecies: The classification just below species. Subspecies live in different geographical areas.

INDEX

For our beloved two-legged pack members: Heidi and Anthony; our grandchildren, Lindsey, Olivia, and Liam; and our four-legged cousins of the wolf, Tony and Bjanka. —JB & JB

RESEARCH AND PHOTOGRAPHY NOTES

Photographing wolves in the Minnesota woods is a lonely experience. Wolves are most active at dusk, through the night, and in the early morning. This means I have to know where they are, get into position to photograph without them knowing I am around, and then sit patiently, sometimes for many hours without making any noise. Just the process of getting into position is difficult.

Temperatures here range from minus 40°F to 100°F (minus 40°C to 40°C). Because of the cold, my cameras sometimes stop working before I do. Since wolves have such a keen sense of smell, I need to be downwind from them or they will quickly leave. They can even detect the scent of mosquito repellent. Any kind of noise will also frighten them away, even just swatting at a mosquito. Sometimes they hear the clicking of the shutter on my cameras.

People often ask if they can go with me to photograph my wolf neighbors, kindly offering to carry my equipment. But I have found that doubling the scents and sounds usually makes my work unsuccessful, which is why I always work alone. After spending many years gaining the trust of several generations of the resident wolf pack, I am now finding it easier to get closer to them than in the past.

Wolves have been an important part of my life for over 30 years. In the early years of my work, when the wolf population was lower, I was lucky to get one good photograph in a year. Now I see them more often, and they aren't as afraid of people because they haven't been hunted in many generations. If you ever want to see a wolf—get up early, go exploring, and be patient and quiet. —JB

ACKNOWLEDGMENTS & CREDITS

I'd like to thank: The Ellesmere and Moose Lake wolf packs for allowing me to become an observer of their complex lives; my friend James Taylor, who in 1989 graciously donated his time and talent to help raise money to fund the Defenders of Wildlife's Wolf Compensation Trust to reimburse ranchers for livestock losses to wolves (a fund that was crucial to the Rocky Mountain reintroduction of wolves); all the biologists and conservationists who have worked endlessly in the fight to protect wolves; and my family, assistants, and employees, who have given me a never-ending amount of support in my career.
—Jim Brandenburg

The publisher gratefully acknowledges the assistance of Christine Kiel, K–3 curriculum and reading consultant; Dr. Luigi Boitani, Department of Animal and Human Biology, University of Rome, Italy, for his expert review of the map on page 11; the U.S. Fish and Wildlife Service, for the maps on page 29; and Kelsey Carlson, education consultant.

Front cover: Face to face with a gray wolf in Nova Scotia, Jim Brandenburg/ Minden Pictures; **Back cover:** (Top) A pair of watchful gray wolves, Jim Brandenburg/Minden Pictures; (Bottom) As Jim Brandenburg takes a break from shooting, a curious arctic wolf checks him out, Stephen Durst

The Library of Congress cataloged the 2008 edition as follows:

Brandenburg, Jim.
  Face to face with wolves / by Jim and Judy Brandenburg.
    p. cm.—(Face to face with animals)
    ISBN 978-1-4263-0242-8 (trade)—
    ISBN 978-1-4263-0243-5 (library)
    1. Wolves—Nunavut—Ellesmere Island. 2. Wolves—Nunavut—Ellesmere Island—Pictorial works. I. Title.
QL737.C22B633 2008
599.773—dc22

2007041217

Text copyright © 2008 James Brandenburg and Judy Brandenburg. Photographs copyright © 2008 James Brandenburg.

First paperback printing 2010
Second paperback printing 2018
2018 paperback edition ISBN:
978-1-4263-3056-8

Pages 5, 22 photographs © Joel Sartore/ National Geographic Creative. Page 21 photograph © Rick Rickman/National Geographic Creative. Page 23 photograph, Judy Brandenburg. Back cover photograph © Stephen Durst/National Geographic Creative.

Since 1888, the National Geographic Society has funded more than 12,000 research, exploration, and preservation projects around the world. The Society receives funds from National Geographic Partners, LLC, funded in part by your purchase. A portion of the proceeds from this book supports this vital work. To learn more, visit natgeo.com/info.

NATIONAL GEOGRAPHIC and Yellow Border Design are trademarks of the National Geographic Society, used under license.

For more information, visit nationalgeographic .com, call 1-800-647-5463, or write to the following address:
National Geographic Partners
1145 17th Street N.W.
Washington, D.C. 20036-4688 U.S.A.

Visit us online at
nationalgeographic.com/books

For librarians and teachers:
ngchildrensbooks.org

More for kids from National Geographic:
kids.nationalgeographic.com

For information about special discounts for bulk purchases, please contact National Geographic Books Special Sales: specialsales@natgeo.com

For rights or permissions inquiries, please contact National Geographic Books Subsidiary Rights: bookrights@natgeo.com

Printed in China
17/RRDS/1